Colors of
GERMANY

by Holly Littlefield
illustrations by Andrea Shine

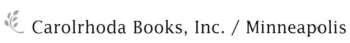

Carolrhoda Books, Inc. / Minneapolis

Map on page 3 by John Erste

Text copyright © 1997 by Carolrhoda Books, Inc.
Illustrations copyright © 1997 by Andrea Shine

This book is available in two editions:
Library binding by Carolrhoda Books, Inc.
Soft cover by First Avenue Editions
c/o The Lerner Publishing Group
241 First Avenue North
Minneapolis, Minnesota 55401 U.S.A.

Library of Congress Cataloging-in-Publication Data

Littlefield, Holly.
  Colors of Germany / by Holly Littlefield ; illustrations by Andrea Shine.
      p.   cm. – (Colors of the world)
  Includes index.
  ISBN 0-87614-887-9 (lib. bdg. : alk. paper)
  ISBN 1-57505-214-8 (pbk. : alk. paper)
  1. Germany—Juvenile literature.   2. Colors—Juvenile literature.
[1. Germany. 2. Color.]   I. Title. II. Series.
DD17.L57 1997
943—dc21   96-29457

Manufactured in the United States of America
1 2 3 4 5 6 – SP – 02 01 00 99 98 97

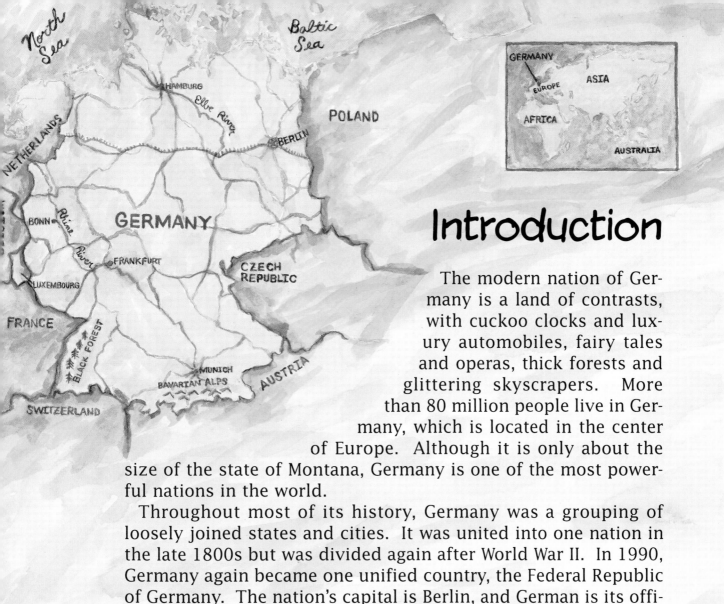

Introduction

The modern nation of Germany is a land of contrasts, with cuckoo clocks and luxury automobiles, fairy tales and operas, thick forests and glittering skyscrapers. More than 80 million people live in Germany, which is located in the center of Europe. Although it is only about the size of the state of Montana, Germany is one of the most powerful nations in the world.

Throughout most of its history, Germany was a grouping of loosely joined states and cities. It was united into one nation in the late 1800s but was divided again after World War II. In 1990, Germany again became one unified country, the Federal Republic of Germany. The nation's capital is Berlin, and German is its official language.

3

White

Weiss (VYS)

The **white** walls of Neuschwanstein Castle rise from a ledge near a beautiful waterfall, with the craggy peaks of the Bavarian Alps all around. The castle, which stands in the southern German state of Bavaria, looks like it belongs in a fairy tale. In fact, it was the model used for the castle in Disney theme parks.

Neuschwanstein Castle was built in the late 1800s by the Bavarian king Ludwig II, who is often called Mad King Ludwig. King Ludwig was not very interested in government. Instead he loved art, music, and architecture. Ludwig spent seventeen years and huge amounts of money building this amazing castle. The Bavarian government feared that the king would use up all of Bavaria's money, so they had Ludwig declared insane and locked up in his castle. Two days later, both the king and his doctor were found dead. They had mysteriously drowned in a nearby lake. The castle was never completed.

5

Yellow

Gelb (GEHLP)

On Christmas Eve, **yellow** candlelight flickers from the branches of traditional German Christmas trees. The custom of decorating evergreen trees with candles, cookies, and ornaments to celebrate Christmas originated hundreds of years ago in Germany and has spread throughout the world.

In Germany, St. Nicholas visits on the night of December 6, rather than on Christmas Eve. He rides a horse from house to house, wearing a long bishop's robe and carrying candy, nuts, and fruit. He leaves these gifts in the shoes and stockings that children have left out for him. Sometimes St. Nicholas comes during the daytime. Then he is usually accompanied by his servant named Ruprecht. While St. Nicholas hands out candy to good children, Ruprecht chases the bad ones with a stick.

Red

Rot (ROHT)

The blood from a **red** dragon named Fafnir gave Siegfried, a hero from German legend, special powers. After Siegfried killed the dragon, weapons were useless against him and he became nearly impossible to defeat. He could also understand the language of the birds. Siegfried stole the dragon's treasure, including a gold ring that gave him even greater powers. Stories about Siegfried, which are more than a thousand years old, are nearly as popular to the Germans as stories of King Arthur are to English-speaking people.

9

10

Brown

Braun (BROWN)

Large, **brown** wooden beams crisscross the fronts of many traditional German houses. The spaces between the beams are filled with brick or with a white material that looks like plaster. This method of building is called half-timber or timber-frame construction. Half-timber construction is extremely sturdy. Some German half-timber houses are more than five hundred years old.

Many towns in Germany were once surrounded by walls. There wasn't much room in these towns for people to build wide houses, so they built tall ones. Many half-timber houses are taller than they are wide. Some houses were built with second and third stories that were larger than the first level and jutted out over the lower walls. This added extra space to a house without taking up too much land inside the city walls.

Silver

Silber (ZIHL-buh)

Carl Benz used **silver**-spoked bicycle tires on his tricar—one of the first practical motorcars. The tricar, which Benz invented in Germany in 1885, looked a bit like an old-fashioned buggy. It had two wheels in the back, a wheel with a steering stick in the front, and a single seat that could hold two people. The motor on the back of the tricar allowed it to go about seven miles per hour. Out of Benz's early automobile company came the modern Daimler-Benz company—maker of Mercedes-Benz cars—which is one of Germany's most important businesses.

Since the early days of Carl Benz's first tricar, the automobile has become increasingly popular with Germans. Their freeway system, called the *Autobahn,* is one of the busiest in the world. There is no speed limit on the *Autobahn,* so drivers can travel as fast as they want. The average speed on German freeways is about 80 miles per hour, but many drivers travel at 120 miles per hour or even faster.

57

13

Pink

Rosa (ROH-zah)

"Nibble, Nibble, like a mouse, who is nibbling at my house?" said the witch, her **pink** eyes gleaming with excitement, when she caught a very hungry Hansel and Gretel eating a piece of her roof. The witch had built her house out of bread and cake and sugar to trap children. Luckily, Hansel and Gretel were able to trick the witch and escape.

The story of Hansel and Gretel is one of more than two hundred German folktales that Jacob and Wilhelm Grimm collected and published. When the Grimm brothers first began collecting these stories in the early 1800s, only a few had ever been written down. Mostly they had just been passed on by word of mouth for generations. Jacob and Wilhelm's written versions of these tales became extremely popular in Germany and in many other countries as well. Many of the world's best-loved fairy tales came from the Grimm brothers' collection, including "Little Red Riding Hood," "Snow White," and "Cinderella."

16

Gold

Gold (GOLT)

Her hair glistens **gold.** Her golden jewelry catches the light. Her voice calls to lonely sailors on passing ships. She is the beautiful but deadly creature from German legend called the Lorelei.

According to the legend, the Lorelei was a water spirit who sat high on a cliff above the Rhine River. As she combed her golden hair, she sang a mysterious song that captured the hearts of all the sailors who heard it. The sailors would steer their ships closer and closer to the Lorelei's cliff, hoping to see the beautiful woman. It is said that many ships crashed on the rocks below the cliff, caught in the Lorelei's treacherous trap.

Green

Grün (GREWN)

In spite of its name, Germany's Black Forest, or Schwarzwald, has **green** trees, just like forests anywhere else in the world. Most of the trees in the forest are fir or spruce, which can look nearly black from a distance. Also, the Black Forest is so dense and the leaves and needles on the trees are so thick that very little light gets through to the forest floor. Even in the middle of the day, the forest can be very dark.

Over one-third of Germany is forestland. The Black Forest is one of the country's largest forests, covering more than a hundred square miles of southwestern Germany. The trees of the forest supply pulp, which is made into paper, and wood, which is used for building and wood carving. This area of Germany is especially known for its beautiful handcarved cuckoo clocks.

Many Germans love to spend time outdoors, hiking and camping. The Black Forest, which is covered with carefully marked hiking trails called *Wanderwege,* is a popular vacation spot.

19

20

Blue

Blau (BLAH-oo)

The **blue** waters of the Rhine River flow for more than eight hundred miles through Germany and five other countries in Europe. It is the busiest river system in the world and one of the most important waterways in Europe. Starting high up in the Swiss Alps, it flows from south to north through Switzerland, Liechtenstein, Austria, France, Germany, and into the Netherlands, where it finally empties into the North Sea.

Ancient castles line the Rhine River in western Germany. During the thirteenth century, many of these castles were controlled by powerful lords who were little more than thieves. They forced every ship that passed to pay a high toll for the use of that part of the river. Often, those who didn't pay were attacked and their ships sunk. The lords became known as robber barons. The robber barons are gone, but many of their castles still remain.

Gray

Grau (GRAOW)

In 1989, the huge, **gray** wall that separated the German city of Berlin into two parts, east and west, came tumbling down. Germany had been divided in two after World War II. One part of the country was called the Federal Republic of Germany, or West Germany. The other part was called the German Democratic Republic, or East Germany. Although Berlin was in East Germany, it was also divided between the two countries.

For nearly thirty years, the people of Berlin lived with a wall dividing their city. Life in West Germany was often easier than life in East Germany. People had more freedoms and a higher standard of living in West Germany. Over the years, many people tried to cross the heavily guarded Berlin Wall and escape from East Germany. Finally, on November 9, 1989, East Germany opened its borders to the west. Thousands crossed from East to West Berlin. Some people danced on top of the wall. Others beat sledgehammers against it and took away pieces for souvenirs as the wall came down. In 1990, Germany was made into one country again.

Index

Alps, 4, 21
Autobahn, 12
Automobiles, 12

Bavaria, 4
Benz, Carl, 12
Berlin, 3, 22
Berlin Wall, 22
Black Forest, 18

Castles, 4, 21
Christmas, 7
Christmas trees, 7
"Cinderella," 14

East Germany (German Democratic
     Republic), 22

Fafnir, 8
Fairy tales, 3, 14

Grimm, Jacob, 14
Grimm, Wilhelm, 14

"Hansel and Gretel," 14
Houses, 11

Language, 3
"Little Red Riding Hood," 14
Location, 3
Lorelei, the, 17
Ludwig II, King, 4

Neuschwanstein Castle, 4

Population, 3

Rhine River, 17, 21
Robber barons, 21
Ruprecht, 7

St. Nicholas, 7
Schwarzwald, 18
Siegfried, 8
Size, 3
"Snow White," 14

Unification, 3, 22

West Germany (Federal Republic of
     Germany), 3, 22
World War II, 3, 22